MY FIRST BOOK OF

MATH AND MYSTERIES

HEATHER O'CONNOR

To order additional copies of this book, contact:
Xlibris
844-714-8691
www.Xlibris.com
Orders@Xlibris.com

ISBN: Softcover   978-1-6698-5863-8
         EBook   978-1-6698-5864-5

Print information available on the last page

Rev. date: 12/28/2022

MATH AND MYSTERIES

My First Book of Math and Mysteries

Mommy made **6** yummy chocolate chip cookies! While they were cooling **2** cookies disappeared!

How many **cookies were left?**

6 cookies - 2 cookies = _____ cookies

Who do you think took the **2 cookies?**

Was it the boy in the **brown pants?**

Was it the girl in the **yellow top?**

Was it the boy in the **gray top**

3

Amy had a pack of **5** color markers. **2** markers are missing!

How many **markers are left?**

5 markers - 2 markers = _____ markers

Who do you think took **the markers?**

Was it the boy in the **green shirt?**

Was it the girl in the **yellow shirt?**

Was it the boy in the **red shirt?**

Max had **4** jars of silver glitter. **2** of the jars are missing.

How many jars of **glitter are left?**

4 jars of glitter – 2 jars of glitter = _____ jars of glitter.

Who do you think took **the glitter?**

Was it the girl with the **red bow in her hair?**

Was it the boy with the **blue baseball cap on?**

Was it the girl with the **yellow bracelet?**

Courtney had **5** yellow flowers in a vase. Someone knocked over the vase and took **2** of the flowers.

How many **flowers are left?**

5 flowers – 2 flowers = _____ flowers

Who do you think took **the flowers?**

Was it the boy in the **green shorts?**

Was it the girl in the **red dress?**

Was it the boy in the **yellow shirt?**

9

Andy bought **4** pieces of pepperoni pizza for him and his friend.

When they opened the box, **2** of the pieces were missing.

How many pieces of **pizza were left?**

4 pieces - 2 pieces =_____ pieces

Who do you think took **the pieces of pizza?**

Was it the boy in the **blue shirt?**

Was it the girl in the **blue shirt?**

Was it the boy in the **green shirt?**

Mandy had **3** jars full of purple paint. When she went to use them **2** were spilled!

How many **jars are still full?**

3 jars of paint - 2 jars of paint = _____ jars of paint

Who do you think **spilled the paint?**

Was it the girl in the **red sweater?**

Was it the boy in the **green shirt?**

Was it the girl with the **yellow dress?**

Printed in the United States
by Baker & Taylor Publisher Services